John Calvin's Illustrated

INSTITUTES

Knowing God & Knowing Ourselves

Book 1: Chapters 1-5

EDITED BY

MARTIN WILLIAMS
& JOY WILLIAMS

ILLUSTRATED BY

PAUL COX

P&R
PUBLISHING
P.O. BOX 817 • PHILLIPSBURG • NEW JERSEY 08865-0817

Text © 2025 by Martin Williams & Joy Williams
Illustrations © 2025 by Paul Cox

ISBN: 979-8-88779-186-9 (print)
ISBN: 979-8-88779-187-6 (ePub)

Printed in the United States of America

Library of Congress Cataloging-in-Publication Data has been applied for.

CONTENTS

TO THE READER

When I first wrote this book, I never expected it to become so popular. At first I kept it short and simple, but when I saw how many people appreciated it, I felt I had to make it **bigger and better** each time I updated it. Even though it took a lot of work, I loved doing it for the church's good.

Last winter, while I was very sick, I worked hard to finish this book, hoping it would be a helpful gift to everyone who believes in God. My only hope and prayer is that it will help and benefit God's church.

My main goal has always been to help the church by **teaching true doctrine**. Even though people have made false accusations against me, I trust that God will help me keep going. My sole aim has always been to benefit the church by upholding the true doctrine of godliness. The devil and his followers will not deter me, for **I trust in God's strength** to persevere.

I wrote this book to guide and teach those who study theology, so that they can read the Bible more easily and understand it better. I believe this book sums up the Christian faith in a way that helps readers know what to look for in Scripture and how to understand it.

If I write any commentaries on the Bible in the future, they'll be brief, because this book covers the big ideas of Scripture. It does this so that readers won't have to go through long explanations and can approach the Bible with the key knowledge they need.

Farewell, kind reader. If my work helps you, please pray for me to God our Father.

Geneva, August 1, 1559

John Calvin

TO KING FRANCIS OF FRANCE

To the Most Mighty and Illustrious Monarch, Francis, Most Christian King of the French, His Sovereign, John Calvin Wishes Peace and Salvation in Christ.

When I started writing this book, I did not plan to present it to Your Majesty. My goal was to provide **basic religious instruction** to help those who are interested in the Christian faith grow in **true godliness**. I especially wanted to help my fellow Frenchmen, many of whom are eager to know Christ but lack proper knowledge of him. This book is written simply and straightforwardly so anyone eager to learn about Christ can understand it.

However, I have seen that certain wicked individuals have caused such chaos in your realm that there is no room for sound doctrine. So I thought it would be useful both to instruct my countrymen and to present Your Majesty with a **clear statement of our beliefs**. This way, you can understand the doctrine that has so enraged these troublemakers who disturb your kingdom with fire and sword. I am not afraid to declare that this book contains the essence of the very doctrine they seek to punish with imprisonment, exile, and even death.

I know these opponents have been spreading false accusations about us, causing you to turn against us. But, as a fair leader, remember that accusations alone are not enough to judge anyone. **Our beliefs have often been condemned** because of our enemies' violent opposition and deceitful slander—not because of any real fault of ours. It is their aggression that leads to unjust punishments without a fair trial and their lies that falsely accuse us of treason and wrongdoing. You, noble King, can see how many lies are told about us daily. They claim our beliefs aim to overthrow governments and cause chaos, but that is far from the truth.

That is why I am asking you to look into this matter closely. I am not worried about my own safety; I am more concerned about the **well-being of all believers and the truth of Christ**, which is being crushed in your kingdom. The real church is being harshly persecuted, and the truth of Christ is being hidden and oppressed. No one is standing up to defend the church against this injustice.

Our beliefs are **grounded in the Bible** and in the **true teachings of Christ**. We are not trying to disrupt society; we are trying to honor God and follow his Word. We respect the early church fathers, and much of what we teach aligns with their writings. But we must remember that **everything belongs to Christ**, and **we must obey him above all else**.

Appealing to long-standing customs instead of the truth is unfair. Sometimes just because a lot of people do something or believe something, it becomes the norm, even if it is wrong. This can make bad actions and mistakes seem acceptable. **True believers should follow God's eternal truth**, not just go along with what everyone else is doing or saying. Isaiah taught us not to fear what others fear but to fear the Lord and honor him as holy. Even if everyone around us is doing or believing the wrong thing, God will still judge them, as he did in the story of Noah. Bad customs are like a disease, and they give us no excuse for ignoring God's truth.

The true church is not always visible, but it endures through Christ's protection. Throughout history, it has often been hidden or oppressed, but **God has always preserved a faithful group**. It is a mistake to focus too much on buildings and leaders, because the church's essence is not in structures or authorities. Only God knows the true form of the church, and believers must trust his will. Even in tough times of persecution, God preserves his church, even if it is hidden.

In conclusion, I urge you, noble King, to **consider the true teachings of the Protestant faith** and protect those who follow it. We believe that if you read this confession with an open mind, you will see the truth and support the cause of the gospel. May the Lord, the King of Kings, establish your throne in righteousness and your rule in fairness.

John Calvin

Basel, August 1535

CHAPTER 1

Knowing God and Knowing Ourselves

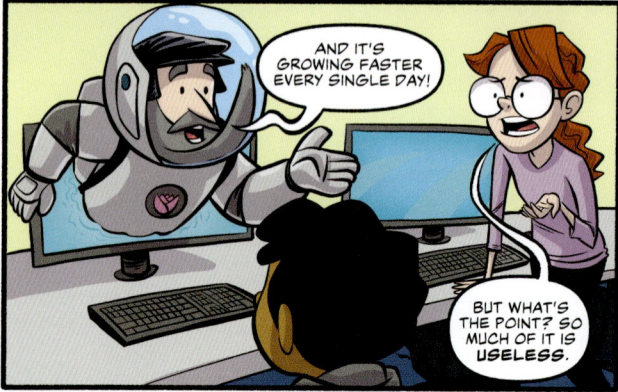

I OBJECT!

I KNOW MYSELF ONLY TOO WELL,

SO WHY DO I NEED TO KNOW GOD IN ORDER TO UNDERSTAND MYSELF?

WITHOUT A **TRUE** KNOWLEDGE OF GOD,

WE CANNOT FULLY GRASP THE REALITY OF OUR OWN SINFUL AND BROKEN CONDITION.

I AM A GOOD AND UPSTANDING PERSON.

IT'S **EASY** TO **THINK** YOU'RE GOOD, BUT WITHOUT KNOWING GOD, WE CAN'T TRULY KNOW OURSELVES.

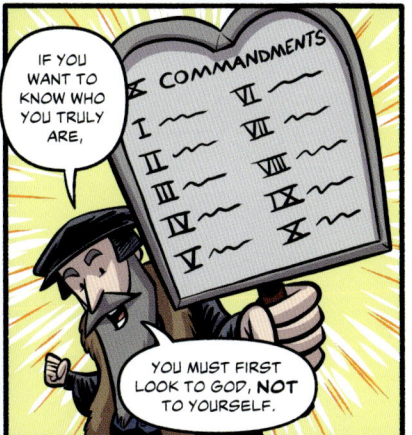

IF YOU WANT TO KNOW WHO YOU TRULY ARE,

COMMANDMENTS

YOU MUST FIRST LOOK TO GOD, **NOT** TO YOURSELF.

DO YOU WANT TO KNOW WHO YOU REALLY ARE?

FIRST, LOOK TO GOD.

THEN, LOOK AT YOURSELF. GOD IS LIKE A **MIRROR** THAT SHOWS US WHO WE TRULY ARE.

WHAT WOULD WE SEE IF WE LOOKED AT OURSELVES IN THE MIRROR OF GOD?

WE WOULD SEE OUR **SINFUL, CORRUPT,** AND **MISERABLE** CONDITION

IN CONTRAST TO THE **MAJESTY** AND **GLORY** OF GOD.

ONLY WHEN WE SEE OURSELVES IN THE MIRROR OF GOD DO WE TRULY RECOGNIZE OUR DEPRAVITY, MISERY, AND UNRIGHTEOUSNESS.

FIRST,

AS FALLEN HUMANS,

WE ARE BY NATURE FULL OF PRIDE.

SECOND,

AS PROUD CREATURES,

WE FLATTER OURSELVES SO MUCH

THAT WE BEGIN TO THINK WE'RE LITTLE GODS!

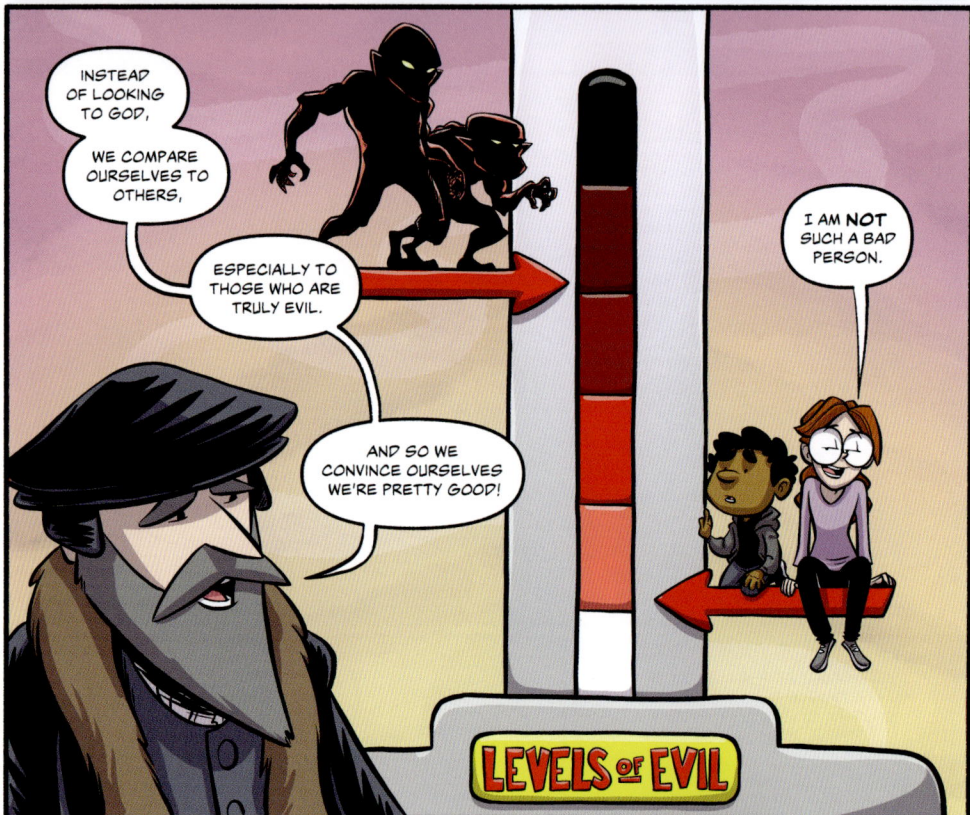

INSTEAD OF LOOKING TO GOD,

WE COMPARE OURSELVES TO OTHERS,

ESPECIALLY TO THOSE WHO ARE TRULY EVIL.

AND SO WE CONVINCE OURSELVES WE'RE PRETTY GOOD!

I AM **NOT** SUCH A BAD PERSON.

LEVELS of EVIL

WHEN WE COMPARE OURSELVES TO OTHERS, WE COME UP LOOKING RELATIVELY CLEAN.

WE ARE JUST LIKE THE PHARISEE IN LUKE 18:11 WHO PRAYED:

"GOD, I THANK YOU THAT I AM **NOT** LIKE OTHER MEN,

EXTORTIONERS, UNJUST, ADULTERERS,

OR EVEN LIKE THIS **TAX COLLECTOR**."

WHEN WE LOOK TO GOD, WHAT DO WE SEE?

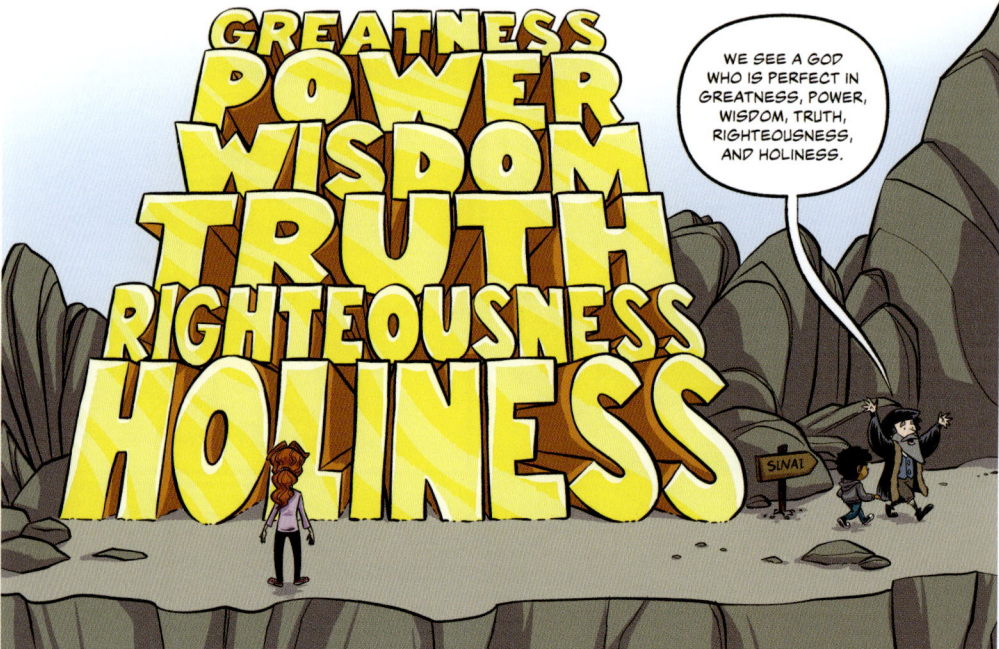

GREATNESS POWER WISDOM TRUTH RIGHTEOUSNESS HOLINESS

WE SEE A GOD WHO IS PERFECT IN GREATNESS, POWER, WISDOM, TRUTH, RIGHTEOUSNESS, AND HOLINESS.

SINAI

AT THE SAME TIME,

WE SEE, BY COMPARISON, OUR OWN LOWLINESS, IGNORANCE, SIN, AND CORRUPTION.

WE BEGIN TO SEE HOW EVEN THINGS THAT ONCE SEEMED GOOD AND RIGHTEOUS

NOW APPEAR WICKED AND EVIL WHEN COMPARED TO THE PURITY AND MAJESTY OF GOD.

AND WE ACKNOWLEDGE WITH THE APOSTLE PAUL:

"I KNOW THAT NOTHING GOOD DWELLS IN ME." (ROMANS 7:18)

UNTIL WE SEE OURSELVES IN THE MIRROR OF GOD'S MAJESTY,

WE'LL NEVER FULLY UNDERSTAND OUR MISERY AND DESPERATE NEED FOR GOD.

GOD, BE MERCIFUL TO ME, A SINNER.

HOW DID GOD'S PEOPLE,

WHO SAW THEMSELVES IN THE MIRROR OF GOD'S MAJESTY AND EXPERIENCED HIS PRESENCE, RESPOND?

DID THEY LEAP FOR JOY?

NO!

THEY RESPONDED LIKE THIS:

"WE SHALL SURELY DIE, FOR WE HAVE SEEN GOD."

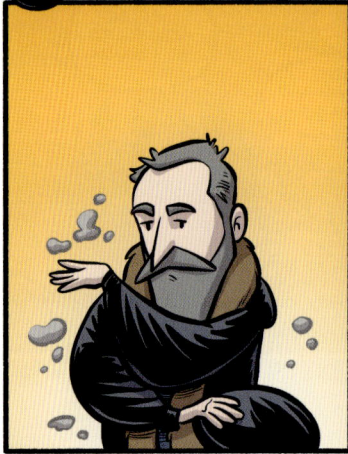

(JUDGES 13:22)

WHY DID THEY REACT IN THIS WAY?

IT WAS BECAUSE THEY SAW THEIR SINFULNESS BEFORE A **HOLY** GOD.

THEREFORE, TRUE HUMILITY COMES ONLY WHEN WE FIRST LOOK TO GOD, AND THEN LOOK AT OURSELVES.

TEN COMM

WHEN GOD APPEARED TO ABRAHAM, ABRAHAM SAID:

I HAVE SPOKEN TO THE LORD,

I WHO AM BUT DUST AND ASHES. (GENESIS 18:27)

ISAIAH CRIED OUT:

"WOE IS ME! FOR I AM LOST;

FOR I AM A MAN OF UNCLEAN LIPS, AND I DWELL IN THE MIDST OF A PEOPLE OF UNCLEAN LIPS;

FOR MY EYES HAVE SEEN THE KING, THE LORD OF HOSTS!" (ISAIAH 6:5)

ELIJAH COULDN'T EVEN APPROACH GOD WITHOUT COVERING HIS FACE WITH HIS CLOAK. (1 KINGS 19:13)

19

ISAIAH DECLARES, "THE MOON WILL BE DISMAYED AND THE SUN ASHAMED WHEN THE LORD ALMIGHTY REIGNS WITH GREAT GLORY." (ISAIAH 24:23)

True wisdom consists of two inseparable parts: knowing God and knowing ourselves. These two types of knowledge are inseparably linked, and we cannot truly understand one without the other.

To truly know ourselves, we must first look at God. His greatness, holiness, and perfection reveal our sinfulness and need. When we see ourselves in the mirror of his majesty, we are struck by the depth of our corruption and misery. This humbling realization leads us to seek God's mercy and grace.

Ultimately, we need to rightly understand both God and ourselves if we want to grow spiritually. Unless we contemplate God's majesty, we remain blind to our flaws and think we are righteous. If we compare ourselves only to others, we deceive ourselves and become proud. But knowledge of God and ourselves forms the foundation of true wisdom: It shapes our purpose, values, and perspective, and it guides us to measure our lives according to his perfect standard.

QUESTIONS FOR DISCUSSION AND MEDITATION

1. What did you learn from this chapter? Describe any ideas, discoveries, or verses that stood out to you.
2. What is the relationship between knowing God and knowing ourselves? Why must these two types of knowledge be linked together?
3. Why does Calvin argue that we cannot truly know ourselves apart from knowing God? What are some practical ways this truth can change how we live?

4. What are the dangers of focusing solely on one of these two types of knowledge without paying attention to the other?

5. What does it mean for us to see ourselves in the mirror of God's majesty? How does God's majesty shape your understanding of your sinfulness and who you truly are?

6. Why is comparing yourself to others unhelpful? What happens when you compare yourself to God instead?

7. When he describes humanity apart from God, Calvin uses strong words like *lowly, ignorant, vain, perverse, corrupt, unrighteous, deceitful, foolish, vile,* and *debased*. Why do people today rarely use this kind of language to describe humanity as a whole? How does downplaying sin impact our culture, the church, and our personal lives?

8. How does Scripture help us understand both who God is and who we are?

9. Look up the following Scripture passages: Genesis 18:27; Judges 6:22–23; Judges 13:22; Isaiah 6:5; Ezekiel 1:28–2:1. How does each person in those passages respond to an encounter with God? What does this tell us about him— and about us?

10. Think of all that happens during a church worship service. What do prayers, songs, confessions, sermons, and other elements of worship tell us about God's majesty and our need for his grace? In what ways could they emphasize his majesty and our need even more?

READ CALVIN FOR YOURSELF!
BOOK 1, CHAPTER 1, SECTIONS 1-3

CHAPTER 2

Knowing God and True Piety

WHAT DOES IT TRULY MEAN TO **KNOW** GOD?

AND WHY IS THIS KNOWLEDGE SO IMPORTANT?

THERE IS A BIG DIFFERENCE BETWEEN JUST KNOWING ABOUT GOD

YOU COULD KNOW A LOT ABOUT GOD,

AND TRULY KNOWING GOD AS OUR HEAVENLY FATHER.

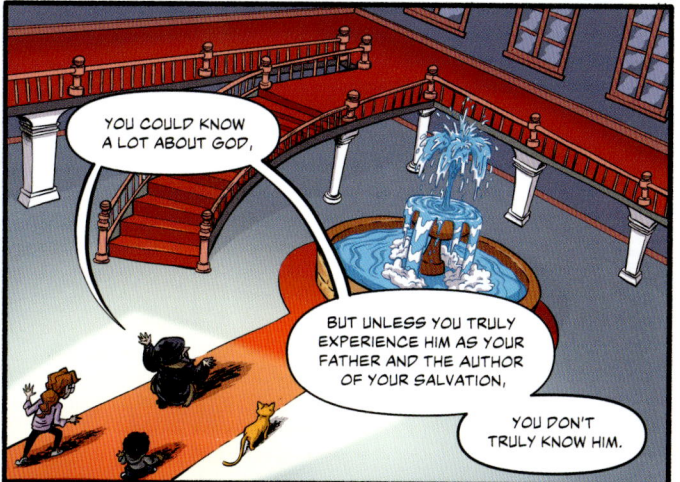

BUT UNLESS YOU TRULY EXPERIENCE HIM AS YOUR FATHER AND THE AUTHOR OF YOUR SALVATION,

YOU DON'T TRULY KNOW HIM.

IT IS NOT ENOUGH TO SIMPLY ACKNOWLEDGE IN YOUR HEAD

THAT THERE'S A GOD WHO CREATED EVERYTHING.

YOU MUST ALSO EXPERIENCE HIM PERSONALLY AS THE FOUNTAIN OF EVERY GOOD THING!

THIS WATER IS **SWEET!**

AND JUST LIKE THIS SWEET WATER, YOU SHOULD FIND ALL YOUR JOY IN HIM,

GIVING THANKS FOR EVERY BLESSING AS A GIFT FROM HIS HAND.

SOME THEOLOGIANS HAVE HEADS FULL OF KNOWLEDGE, BUT HEARTS THAT ARE COLD AND EMPTY...

...WHILE MANY ORDINARY CHRISTIANS HAVE A GENUINE KNOWLEDGE OF GOD BECAUSE THEY JOIN IT WITH TRUE PIETY.

SOME PEOPLE THINK OF PIETY AS STANDING IN FRONT OF THE CHURCH, PRAYING LONG, ELOQUENT PRAYERS.

OTHERS ASSOCIATE PIETY WITH PUTTING LOTS OF MONEY IN THE OFFERING PLATE.

BUT THAT'S NOT **TRUE** PIETY.

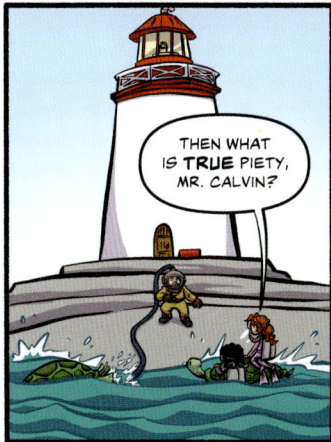

THEN WHAT IS **TRUE** PIETY, MR. CALVIN?

TRUE PIETY IS A **REVERENCE** FOR GOD JOINED WITH **LOVE** FOR HIM.

29

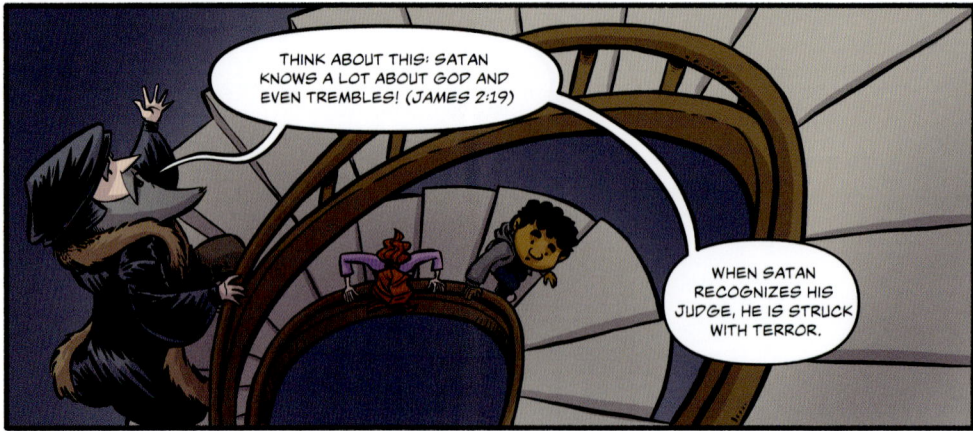

THINK ABOUT THIS: SATAN KNOWS A LOT ABOUT GOD AND EVEN TREMBLES! (JAMES 2:19)

WHEN SATAN RECOGNIZES HIS JUDGE, HE IS STRUCK WITH TERROR.

BUT WHILE SATAN KNOWS A LOT ABOUT GOD AND EVEN TREMBLES AT THE THOUGHT OF HIM, HE DOESN'T **LOVE** GOD.

THAT'S WHY FEAR WITHOUT LOVE ISN'T TRUE PIETY, AND LOVE WITHOUT FEAR ISN'T TRUE PIETY EITHER.

GOD'S CHILDREN, HOWEVER, BOTH FEAR AND LOVE HIM AT THE SAME TIME.

MOREOVER, THEIR FEAR, UNLIKE SATAN'S, ISN'T THE FEAR OF JUDGMENT

ON

OFF

RATHER, IT'S A **REVERENT** FEAR THAT'S JOINED WITH LOVE FOR GOD.

THIS IS BECAUSE THEY KNOW GOD AS THEIR HEAVENLY FATHER, WHO CARES FOR THEM, PROTECTS THEM, GUIDES THEM, AND PROVIDES THEM WITH EVERY GOOD THING.

BUT SOME PEOPLE GET CAUGHT UP IN SPECULATIVE, AND OFTEN EMPTY, QUESTIONS.

IF GOD MADE THE WORLD, THEN WHO MADE GOD?

WHAT WAS GOD DOING BEFORE HE MADE THE WORLD?

IF GOD CAN DO ALL THINGS, CAN HE MAKE A ROCK SO BIG HE CAN'T MOVE IT?

WHY DID GOD MAKE MOSQUITOES?

THESE KINDS OF QUESTIONS ARE NOTHING MORE THAN IDLE SPECULATIONS ABOUT GOD.

YOU WHO CHASE AFTER EMPTY QUESTIONS, STOP AND WAKE UP TO WHAT **REALLY** MATTERS!

WHAT WE REALLY NEED TO WRESTLE WITH ISN'T EMPTY QUESTIONS OR IDLE SPECULATIONS ABOUT GOD.

INSTEAD, WE SHOULD ASK **OURSELVES** QUESTIONS LIKE THESE:

WHAT IS GOD LIKE?

WHAT IS GOD'S WILL FOR MY LIFE?

HOW CAN I SERVE GOD WITH MY LIFE?

HOW CAN I LIVE FOR GOD'S GLORY?

32

THEREFORE, THEY ARE CONSTANTLY AT WAR WITH THEIR WORLDLY HABITS.

THEY DO THIS NOT OUT OF FEAR OF GOD'S JUDGMENT...

...BUT BECAUSE THEY LOVE AND REVERE GOD AS FATHER, WORSHIPING AND ADORING HIM AS LORD.

GENUINE WORSHIP EXISTS ONLY WHEN THE KNOWLEDGE OF GOD IS JOINED WITH TRUE PIETY.

GOD IS LOOKING FOR TRUE WORSHIPERS WHO WORSHIP HIM WITH SINCERE HEARTS.

CHAPTER SUMMARY

There is a significant difference between knowing about God and knowing God personally as our heavenly Father. True knowledge of God is not merely intellectual or theoretical; it is profoundly personal and relational. Those who know God in this way experience him as the fountain of every good thing and as a loving Father who cares deeply for us. This knowledge requires true piety, which Calvin defines as a genuine love and deep reverence for God.

The purpose of knowing God is to teach us fear and reverence, so that we seek every good thing from him with thankful hearts. When we know God, we are able to rely completely on him for everything, because we recognize that we are sustained by his grace alone. Ultimately, this draws us to worship God with sincere hearts that fully trust in his loving care and provision.

QUESTIONS FOR DISCUSSION AND MEDITATION

1. What is the difference between knowing *about* God and knowing God *personally* as our heavenly Father? Why is a personal experience of God important?
2. How does the image of a fountain help illustrate our need to personally experience God? Why is it important for us to experience him as the fountain of every good thing, and how does experiencing him in this way impact our daily lives and choices?
3. How does Calvin define "true piety"? What is the connection between true piety and knowing God?

4. Why is it important for us to know God personally, and how does this knowledge transform our relationship with him?
5. What is the right fear of God? How does it relate to a love for God? Why are both of these things essential aspects of a true relationship with him?
6. What is the difference between serving God out of fear of his judgment and serving him because you love and revere him as your Father? How does our attitude toward God shape the way we approach and relate to him? What motivates *you* to serve and obey God?
7. What are idle speculations about God? Why does Calvin caution us against making them? What does he say we should prioritize instead?
8. How should a child of God approach him in times of trouble? What difference does it make when you trust in his care?
9. Do you seek your happiness in God or in the things of this world? How do you think seeking your happiness in God could help you serve, worship, and obey him better?
10. What does it mean to worship God with a sincere heart, and how can we practice "true worship" in our daily lives?

READ CALVIN FOR YOURSELF!
BOOK 1, CHAPTER 2, SECTIONS 1-2

CHAPTER 3

The Seed of Religion in Every Heart

MOST HIGH COURT

A MAN DIED AND STOOD BEFORE THE JUDGMENT SEAT OF GOD.

GOD, IN HIS PERFECT HOLINESS, DECLARED HIM GUILTY AND SENTENCED HIM TO ETERNAL PUNISHMENT IN HELL.

HE CRIED OUT, PROTESTING THAT HE HAD BEEN UNFAIRLY JUDGED BY GOD.

WAIT—THIS CAN'T BE RIGHT!

WHY AM I BEING CONDEMNED?

I'VE LIVED A GOOD LIFE!

I'VE TRIED TO BE KIND TO EVERYONE!

IT'S JUST NOT FAIR!

IT'S NOT THAT I DIDN'T WANT TO BELIEVE IN GOD.

NO ONE EVER TOLD ME ABOUT HIM.

HOW COULD I BELIEVE IN SOMEONE I'VE NEVER EVEN HEARD OF?

WHAT WOULD HAPPEN TO SOMEONE LIKE THAT?

THEY WOULD STILL FACE GOD'S JUDGMENT AND ETERNAL PUNISHMENT.

BUT WHY WOULD GOD JUDGE SOMEONE WHO NEVER HAD A CHANCE TO HEAR ABOUT HIM?

BECAUSE AN AWARENESS OF GOD IS PLANTED IN THE HEART OF EVERY PERSON.

TO PREVENT PEOPLE FROM MAKING EXCUSES...

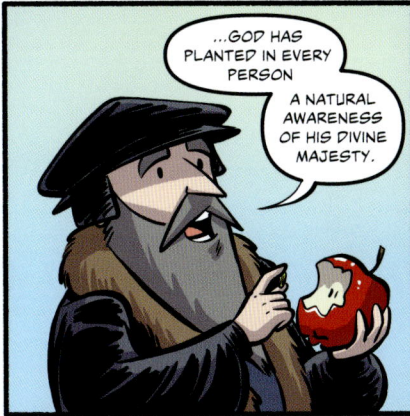

...GOD HAS PLANTED IN EVERY PERSON A NATURAL AWARENESS OF HIS DIVINE MAJESTY.

EVEN THOUGH PEOPLE HAVE THIS KNOWLEDGE, THEY REFUSE TO HONOR GOD OR OBEY HIM. IT IS THIS REJECTION THAT CONDEMNS THEM.

AS THE APOSTLE PAUL SAYS IN ROMANS 1:20-21:

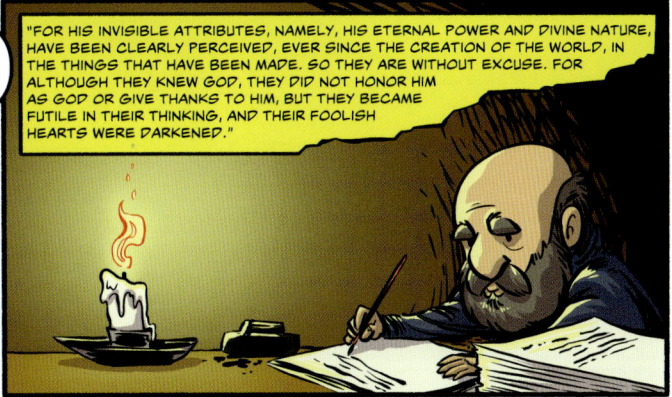

"FOR HIS INVISIBLE ATTRIBUTES, NAMELY, HIS ETERNAL POWER AND DIVINE NATURE, HAVE BEEN CLEARLY PERCEIVED, EVER SINCE THE CREATION OF THE WORLD, IN THE THINGS THAT HAVE BEEN MADE. SO THEY ARE WITHOUT EXCUSE. FOR ALTHOUGH THEY KNEW GOD, THEY DID NOT HONOR HIM AS GOD OR GIVE THANKS TO HIM, BUT THEY BECAME FUTILE IN THEIR THINKING, AND THEIR FOOLISH HEARTS WERE DARKENED."

I CALL THIS AWARENESS OF THEIR CREATOR THE "SEED OF RELIGION."

WHAT IS THE SEED OF RELIGION?

MMMM... THERE MUST BE A WISE AND POWERFUL BEING BEHIND ALL OF THIS.

EVERY PERSON IS BORN WITH A NATURAL AWARENESS OF GOD— A SENSE THAT HE EXISTS AND CREATED EVERYTHING.

AS I EXPLAINED BEFORE, THE "SEED OF RELIGION" IS THE NATURAL AWARENESS OF GOD, DIVINELY PLANTED IN THE HEART OF EVERY PERSON.

...ABOUT THE PEOPLE LIVING IN THE MOST DISTANT CORNERS OF THE EARTH.

THINK FOR A MOMENT...

EVEN THOUGH THEY'VE NEVER HEARD OF THE TRUE GOD, THEY STILL HAVE THEIR OWN RELIGIONS, DON'T THEY?

WHY IS THAT?

BECAUSE GOD HAS IMPRINTED THE KNOWLEDGE OF HIMSELF ON EVERY HUMAN HEART.

CONSIDER THIS: WHY DO YOU THINK THE WORLD IS SO FULL OF IDOLS?

IT'S BECAUSE WE WERE MADE TO KNOW, LOVE, ENJOY, AND WORSHIP GOD.

BUT INSTEAD OF WORSHIPING THE TRUE GOD,

PEOPLE TRY TO FILL THE EMPTY SPACE INSIDE THEM—THE SPACE THAT WAS MADE FOR GOD—WITH IDOLS.

WHAT EXACTLY IS AN IDOL?

AN IDOL IS ANYTHING YOU LOVE, TRUST, AND OBEY MORE THAN GOD.

ANYTHING OR ANYONE THAT CONSUMES MORE OF YOUR THOUGHTS, PASSIONS, TIME, ENERGY, OR MONEY THAN GOD IS AN IDOL.

IDOLATRY SHOWS US CLEARLY THAT AN AWARENESS OF GOD IS IMPRINTED ON EVERY PERSON'S HEART.

HOW ELSE CAN YOU EXPLAIN WHY PEOPLE ARE SO EAGER TO WORSHIP SOMEONE OR SOMETHING, RATHER THAN TO LIVE WITHOUT GOD AT ALL?

SOME MIGHT SAY,

"RELIGION IS JUST THE INVENTION OF SOME CLEVER PEOPLE."

"THEY USE IT ONLY TO MANIPULATE AND CONTROL OTHERS."

RELIGION

RELIGION

41

YES, IT'S TRUE, SOME PEOPLE DO USE RELIGION TO MANIPULATE AND CONTROL OTHERS.

BUT THEY COULD NEVER SUCCEED IN THIS IF THE KNOWLEDGE OF GOD WEREN'T ALREADY PLANTED IN THE HUMAN HEART.

THERE MUST FIRST BE A SEED FOR A PLANT TO GROW.

IN THE SAME WAY,

ALL RELIGIONS IN THE WORLD ARE PROOF OF THE SEED OF RELIGION THAT GOD HAS FIRMLY PLANTED IN EVERY MIND.

BOTH THE ONE WHO INVENTS A RELIGION...

...AND THE ONE WHO FOLLOWS IT...

...ARE CLEAR EVIDENCE OF THE SEED OF RELIGION THAT GOD HAS PLANTED IN ALL PEOPLE.

NO ONE DESPISED THE GODS MORE OR SPOKE AGAINST THEM WITH GREATER CONTEMPT THAN THE WICKED ROMAN EMPEROR, GAIUS CALIGULA.

WHERE IS THIS SO-CALLED GOD?

YOU **FOOLISH** PEOPLE! HOW CAN YOU BELIEVE IN A GOD THAT DOESN'T EVEN EXIST?

YET CALIGULA WAS SO TERRIFIED BY LIGHTNING STORMS THAT HE WOULD JUMP OUT OF HIS BED AND HIDE UNDER IT, TRYING TO ESCAPE THE WRATH OF THE GOD HE CLAIMED DIDN'T EXIST.

THERE ARE OTHERS LIKE HIM, WHO BOLDLY MOCK GOD AND YET TREMBLE AT THE SLIGHTEST SIGN OF DANGER, EVEN AT SOMETHING AS SMALL AS THE RUSTLING OF A LEAF. (LEVITICUS 26:36)

WHAT IS THE CAUSE OF THIS FEAR?

IT'S BECAUSE GOD TERRIFIES THEIR CONSCIENCES,

FILLING THEM WITH A DEEP AWARENESS OF HIS DIVINE MAJESTY AND RIGHTEOUS JUDGMENT AGAINST THEIR SIN.

THIS FEAR DRIVES PEOPLE TO HIDE,

SEEKING DISTRACTIONS AND TEMPORARY ESCAPES— WHETHER THROUGH WORK,

ENTERTAINMENT,

FOOD,

ALCOHOL, DRUGS, OR ANYTHING ELSE—

TO FLEE FROM THE PRESENCE OF GOD AND BLOT OUT ANY AWARENESS OF HIM.

43

AND ALTHOUGH THIS AWARENESS OF GOD MIGHT SEEM TO VANISH FOR A TIME...

...IT INEVITABLY RETURNS WITH NEW FORCE

BECAUSE GOD HAS PLANTED IT DEEP IN THEIR MINDS.

EVEN WHEN PEOPLE TRY TO CAST THE KNOWLEDGE OF GOD AWAY, THEY CAN NEVER TRULY ESCAPE IT.

THEIR CONSCIENCES TREMBLE WITH ANXIETY AND GNAW AT THEM LIKE A WORM EATING ITS WAY THROUGH AN APPLE.

IN FACT, THE MORE THEY TRY TO RID THEMSELVES OF THE KNOWLEDGE OF GOD, THE MORE IT GROWS STRONGER AND THRIVES.

WHY IS THIS?

BECAUSE THIS KNOWLEDGE IS NOT SOMETHING TAUGHT IN SCHOOL...

...BUT RATHER SOMETHING GOD HAS FIRMLY PLANTED IN EVERY PERSON'S HEART FROM THE MOMENT THEY WERE BORN.

ALL PEOPLE ARE CREATED FOR THE PURPOSE OF KNOWING GOD. EVEN THE PAGAN PHILOSOPHERS HAVE ACKNOWLEDGED THIS TRUTH.

BIG BOOK OF PHILOSOPHY

THE ANCIENT PHILOSOPHER PLATO SHOWS HOW HUMANITY NATURALLY SENSES THE EXISTENCE OF GOD.

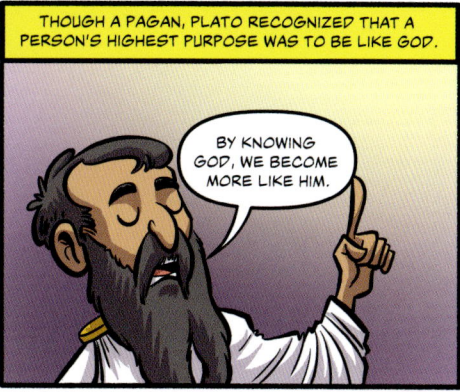

THOUGH A PAGAN, PLATO RECOGNIZED THAT A PERSON'S HIGHEST PURPOSE WAS TO BE LIKE GOD.

BY KNOWING GOD, WE BECOME MORE LIKE HIM.

HOW COULD PLATO THINK THAT IF HE WASN'T A CHRISTIAN?

BECAUSE THE KNOWLEDGE OF GOD IS IMPRINTED ON EVERY HUMAN HEART.

ANOTHER EXAMPLE IS THE GREEK HISTORIAN PLUTARCH, WHO WROTE A FICTIONAL DIALOGUE BETWEEN THE HERO ODYSSEUS AND AN ENCHANTED PIG NAMED GRYLLUS.

IN THE STORY, GRYLLUS SAYS TO ODYSSEUS:

PEOPLE WHO REJECT RELIGION ARE NO BETTER THAN ANIMALS.

IN FACT, THEY'RE EVEN WORSE—

THEY COMMIT ALL KINDS OF EVIL AND LIVE RESTLESS, UNFULFILLED LIVES.

WHAT SETS HUMANS APART FROM ANIMALS IS THEIR ABILITY TO KNOW AND WORSHIP GOD.

45

QUESTIONS FOR DISCUSSION AND MEDITATION

1. What does it mean that every person has a "seed of religion" planted in their heart? What are the implications of this?

2. What evidence does Calvin provide to support his claim that every person has a natural awareness of God? How do you see this play out in today's world?

3. Why do people suppress their knowledge of God, and in what ways do they do so?

4. What is idolatry? How does it prove that humanity has a natural awareness of God? What does it reveal about human nature and our deep desire to worship someone or something?

5. How would Calvin respond to the argument that religion is merely a human invention designed for social or moral control?

6. People often ask, "What about those who have never heard of God? Is it fair for God to judge them?" How does this chapter help answer that question?

7. What support does Romans 1:18–2:6 lend to Calvin's teaching about humanity's natural awareness of God? Why, according to Romans 1:20, are all people "without excuse"? Consider key phrases that Paul goes on to use throughout that passage, such as "exchanged" (vv. 23, 25, 26), "therefore" (v. 24), "for this reason" (v. 26), and "the work of the law . . . written on their hearts" (Romans 2:15).

8. How does Calvin describe people's attempts to block out their awareness of God? Why do these efforts ultimately fail, and how does our contemporary society reflect this internal conflict?

9. Calvin observes that the more someone tries to suppress their knowledge of God, the stronger it becomes. What does this reveal about humanity's ultimate purpose in life?

10. What distinguishes humans from animals, and what does this difference reveal about the unique purpose that human beings have been given?

READ CALVIN FOR YOURSELF!
BOOK 1, CHAPTER 3, SECTIONS 1–3

CHAPTER 4
The Corrupted Seed of Religion

GOD HAS PLANTED A SEED OF RELIGION IN THE HEARTS OF ALL PEOPLE.

WHAT HAPPENED TO THAT SEED?

DID IT GROW INTO SOMETHING BEAUTIFUL AND BEAR GOOD FRUIT?

SADLY, SIN HAS CORRUPTED THE SEED. INSTEAD OF PRODUCING GOOD FRUIT, IT NOW BEARS EVIL FRUIT.

ALL HUMANITY HAS TURNED AWAY FROM THE TRUE KNOWLEDGE OF GOD, AND AS A RESULT, TRUE PIETY HAS VANISHED FROM THE WORLD.

49

WHILE GOD HAS PLANTED THE SEED OF RELIGION IN EVERY HUMAN HEART...

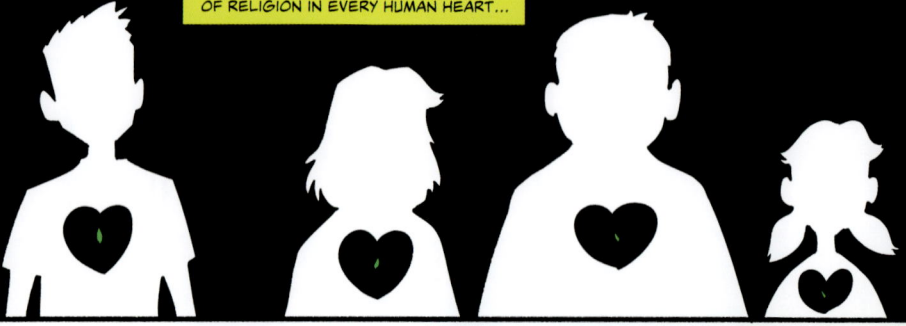

...HARDLY ANYONE NURTURES IT.

THE TRUTH IS, THERE'S NO ONE IN WHOM THIS SEED TRULY TAKES ROOT AND BEARS GOOD FRUIT.

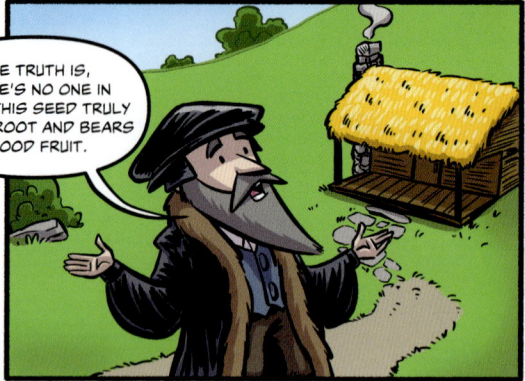

WHAT? THERE IS NO ONE?

HOW CAN THAT BE TRUE?

WE'LL EXPLORE WHY THIS HAPPENS IN BOOK 2.

FOR NOW, LET'S SEE WHAT KIND OF FRUIT GROWS FROM THIS CORRUPTED SEED.

SUPERSTITION

PRACTICAL ATHEISM

FALSE ZEAL

HYPOCRISY

SUPERSTITION, PRACTICAL ATHEISM, FALSE ZEAL, AND HYPOCRISY.

THE FIRST FRUIT THAT COMES FROM THE CORRUPTED SEED OF RELIGION IS **SUPERSTITION.**

WHAT IS SUPERSTITION?

SUPERSTITION IS A BELIEF OR PRACTICE THAT HAS NO BASIS IN TRUTH.

FOR EXAMPLE, SOME PEOPLE BELIEVE THAT BLACK CATS BRING BAD LUCK.

ARE YOU TALKING ABOUT THAT KIND OF SUPERSTITION?

NOT EXACTLY! THAT'S A SUPERSTITION, BUT I'M TALKING ABOUT SOMETHING FAR MORE SERIOUS.

SUPERSTITION IS WHEN PEOPLE REFUSE TO KNOW GOD AS HE HAS REVEALED HIMSELF IN HIS WORD...

HOLY BIBLE

...AND INSTEAD FASHION A GOD OUT OF THEIR OWN IMAGINATION.

AS A RESULT, THE SUPERSTITIOUS DON'T WORSHIP THE ONE **TRUE** GOD...

...BUT RATHER WORSHIP AN IMAGINARY GOD—AN INVENTION OF THEIR OWN CORRUPT HEARTS AND MINDS.

IN ROMANS 1:21-22, PAUL DESCRIBES THIS TWISTED REASONING:

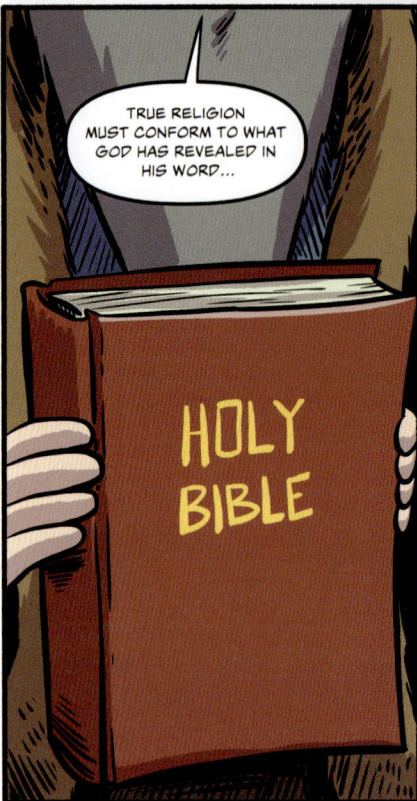

"THEY BECAME FUTILE IN THEIR THINKING, AND THEIR FOOLISH HEARTS WERE DARKENED.

CLAIMING TO BE WISE, THEY BECAME FOOLS."

SUPERSTITION

FAL... ZEA...

...YPOCRISY

TRUE RELIGION MUST CONFORM TO WHAT GOD HAS REVEALED IN HIS WORD...

HOLY BIBLE

...FOR GOD ALWAYS REMAINS TRUE TO HIMSELF AND DOESN'T CHANGE ACCORDING TO THE DESIRES OR VAIN IMAGINATIONS OF SINFUL HUMANS.

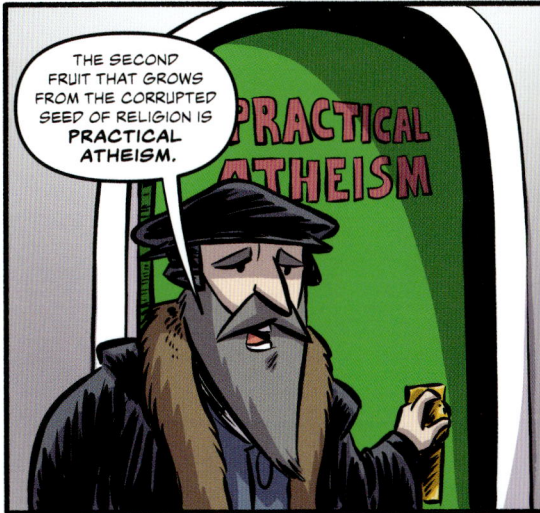

HOWEVER, THE KNOWLEDGE OF GOD, ENGRAVED UPON EVERY HUMAN HEART, CAN NEVER BE ERASED...

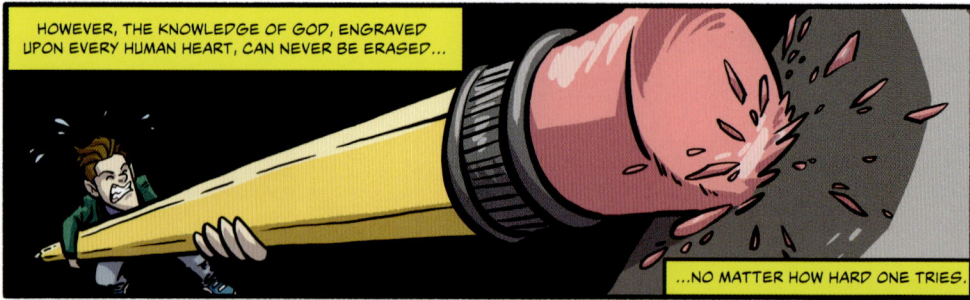

...NO MATTER HOW HARD ONE TRIES.

BUT EVEN IF PEOPLE DO NOT COMPLETELY DENY THE EXISTENCE OF GOD, THEY ACT AS IF HE'S LOCKED AWAY IN HEAVEN BY DENYING HIS POWER AND PROVIDENCE IN THE WORLD.

SURE, GOD MIGHT BE REAL, BUT HE DOESN'T ACTUALLY CONTROL WHAT HAPPENS DOWN HERE.

THEY MIGHT ADMIT THERE'S A GOD, BUT THEY STRIP HIM OF HIS MAJESTY BY DENYING HIS POWER AND PROVIDENCE—LIKE SOMEONE TRYING TO BLOCK OUT THE SUN WITH THEIR HANDS AS IF THAT COULD MAKE IT DISAPPEAR.

EVEN WORSE, THEY OUTRIGHT REJECT GOD'S JUST JUDGMENT OF THE WICKED.

I BELIEVE IN A HIGHER POWER, BUT A GOD OF JUDGMENT? NO WAY!

YEAH, IF GOD IS JUST, WHY DOES SO MUCH EVIL GO UNPUNISHED?

WHOA, THAT'S UNBELIEVABLY **WRONG!**

TO ACKNOWLEDGE GOD'S EXISTENCE BUT DENY HIS JUDGMENT

IS TO TURN HIM INTO A DEAD AND EMPTY IDOL.

IN THE END, THIS IS NO DIFFERENT FROM FLATLY DENYING THAT GOD EXISTS.

BUT WHY WOULD SOMEONE BELIEVE IN GOD BUT REJECT HIS JUDGMENT?

IT'S BECAUSE THEY WANT TO FREELY INDULGE IN SINFUL PLEASURES WITHOUT FEARING GOD'S JUDGMENT.

STILL, NO ONE CAN COMPLETELY DENY GOD, NO MATTER HOW HARD THEY TRY.

IT'S LIKE CLOSING OUR EYES TIGHTLY ON A SUNNY DAY AND SAYING, "THERE'S NO SUN."

HOW **SILLY!**

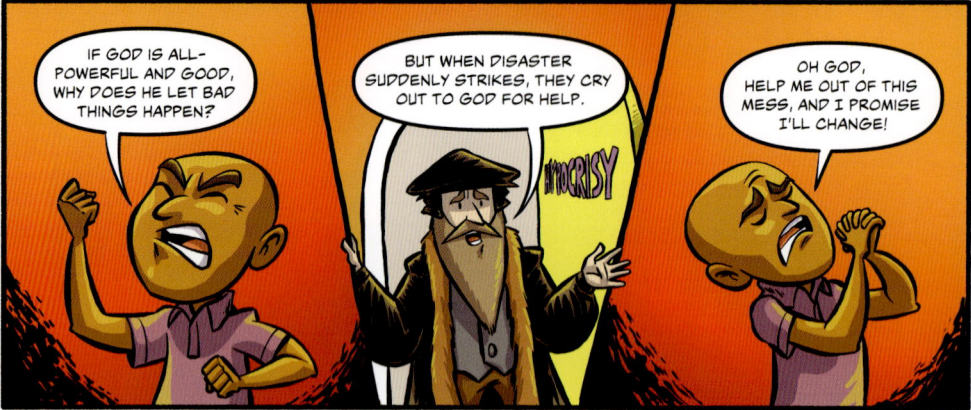

THEY DON'T TRULY SEEK GOD OR WORSHIP HIM OUT OF LOVE AND REVERENCE.

INSTEAD, THEY ONLY FEAR HIS JUDGMENT.

RATHER THAN SERVING GOD WITH INTEGRITY OF HEART AND HOLINESS OF LIFE...

...THEY TRY TO EARN GOD'S FAVOR WITH EMPTY, OUTWARD ACTS OF RELIGIOUS DEVOTION.

THIS IS PURE HYPOCRISY.

INSTEAD OF RELYING ON GOD,

THEY PUT THEIR TRUST IN HOLLOW RITUALS AND EMPTY CEREMONIES THAT HAVE NO TRUE MEANING.

IN THE END, THEY BECOME ENTANGLED IN A WEB OF LIES,

WHERE THE DARKNESS OF THEIR WICKEDNESS GROWS SO THICK THAT IT SUFFOCATES ANY AWARENESS OF GOD.

BUT EVEN SO, THEIR BELIEF IN GOD REMAINS, LIKE A SEED THAT CAN NEVER BE FULLY UPROOTED.

YET THIS SEED IS SO CORRUPTED THAT IT PRODUCES ONLY THE MOST ROTTEN KIND OF FRUIT.

60

CHAPTER SUMMARY

By planting a "seed of religion" in every human heart, God ensures that all people have a natural awareness of him. This awareness is meant to lead them to worship him. However, sin has corrupted the seed and prevented it from producing the good fruit of genuine devotion and true piety. Instead, it bears rotten fruit that leads humanity away from truly knowing God and worshiping him alone.

The four rotten fruits of the corrupted seed are superstition, practical atheism, false zeal, and hypocrisy. *Superstition* occurs when people reject the true God who is revealed in Scripture and invent gods based on their own imaginations. *Practical atheism* is seen when people live as if God doesn't exist—denying his providence and judgment—despite claiming to believe in him. *False zeal* arises when people passionately pursue religion without having a true knowledge of God, which leads them to worship gods of their own imagination. *Hypocrisy* occurs when people do not truly love or revere God but instead perform outward religious acts because they fear judgment, relying on these empty rituals instead of on genuine faith.

Despite the ways it has been corrupted, an awareness of God remains deeply ingrained in every human heart and cannot be fully erased. However, unless it is nurtured by the truth that God reveals to us in the Bible, this seed can produce only rotten fruits. True religion must be founded on God's revelation in Scripture; anything apart from this leads to error, idolatry, and spiritual ruin.

READ CALVIN FOR YOURSELF!
BOOK 1, CHAPTER 4, SECTIONS 1–4

QUESTIONS FOR DISCUSSION AND MEDITATION

1. How has sin corrupted the "seed of religion" in our hearts, and how does this corruption affect our ability to worship God truly and be genuinely devoted to him?

2. What is Calvin's definition of *superstition*? What are some superstitions, as he defines them, that you see people hold today?

3. Why do people invent gods based on their own imaginations instead of worshiping the one true God? What dangers follow from this?

4. In your own words, what is practical atheism? What does it look like for someone to live as if God doesn't exist? Why is practical atheism a risk even for professing Christians?

5. Why is it dangerous to have zeal for religion without truly knowing God? How can we make sure that our worship is grounded in God's truth that is revealed in Scripture?

6. Why does Calvin reject the view that, as long as someone is sincere, it doesn't really matter what they believe?

7. Why do some people engage in religious practices without truly loving or revering God? How might we detect hypocrisy in others? How can we guard against it in our own lives?

8. Sometimes people say, "All religions and philosophies lead to the same God." What does Calvin say to this idea? What does he argue that people are worshiping when they create idols?

9. Why is it impossible to uproot people's "seed of religion"? How can this seed still point people toward God even though it is corrupted by sin?

10. What practical steps can you take to cultivate true piety and to actively guard your own life against corrupting fruits?

CHAPTER 5
Knowing God Through Creation and Providence

64

FIRST, GOD HAS REVEALED HIMSELF IN THE WHOLE DESIGN OF THE UNIVERSE.

THE SUN, MOON, PLANETS, STARS, GALAXIES...

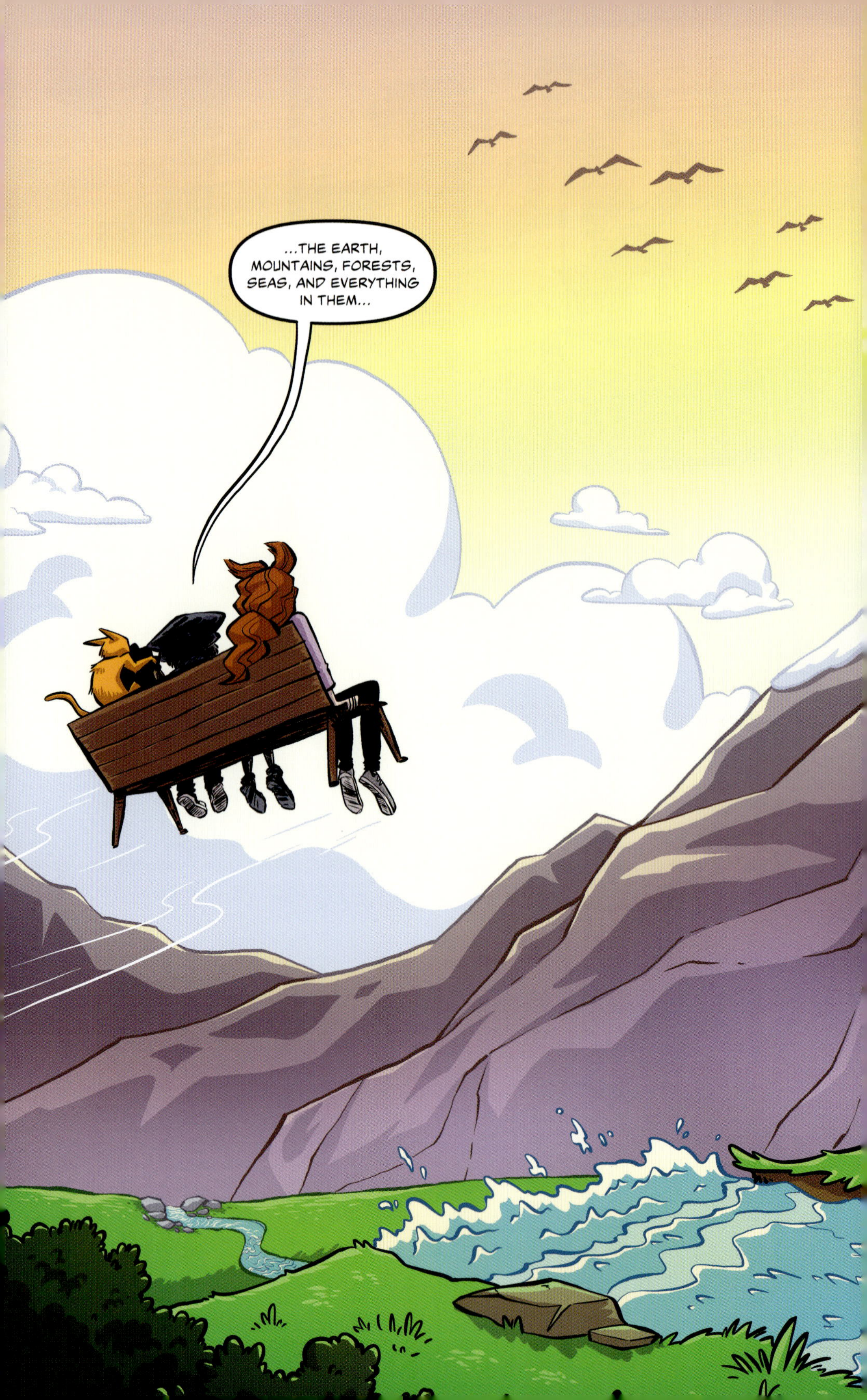
...THE EARTH, MOUNTAINS, FORESTS, SEAS, AND EVERYTHING IN THEM...

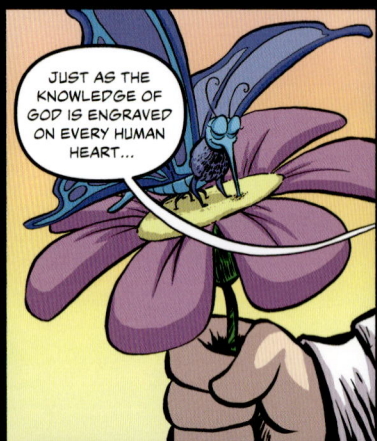

FIRST,

REMEMBER, KIDS, GOD HAS REVEALED HIMSELF IN THE CREATION OF THE UNIVERSE.

SECOND, GOD HAS REVEALED HIMSELF NOT ONLY IN CREATION BUT ALSO IN HIS PROVIDENCE!

LET ME EXPLAIN WHAT I MEAN BY PROVIDENCE.

GOD'S PROVIDENCE MEANS HE UPHOLDS AND GOVERNS THE WORLD WITH UNCEASING CARE.

NOTHING HAPPENS BY CHANCE!

FOR EXAMPLE, HE SETS THE BOUNDARIES OF THE SEAS, COMMANDING THE WATERS WHERE TO STOP.

HE DIRECTS THE MOVEMENTS OF THE PLANETS AND STARS, KEEPING THEM IN PERFECT ORDER.

HE GOVERNS THE SEASONS, THE DAYS, AND THE YEARS, SUSTAINING EVERYTHING BY HIS POWER!

BUT **NOTHING** IS TRULY RANDOM!

GOD GOVERNS ALL THINGS BY HIS PROVIDENCE.

WHAT SEEMS LIKE CHANCE IS ACTUALLY PART OF HIS WISE AND FATHERLY CARE.

IN HIS PROVIDENCE, GOD SHOWS KINDNESS AND GENEROSITY TO ALL.

AT THE SAME TIME,

HE UPHOLDS JUSTICE BY CARING FOR HIS PEOPLE AND JUDGING THE WICKED.

HUMAN HISTORY BEARS WITNESS TO GOD'S PROVIDENTIAL CARE FOR HIS PEOPLE AND HIS RIGHTEOUS JUDGMENT OF THE WICKED.

JAMES 4:6 TELLS US: "GOD OPPOSES THE PROUD BUT GIVES GRACE TO THE HUMBLE."

THIS SHOWS THAT GOD IS A GOD OF JUSTICE!

BUT HOLD ON!

IF THAT'S TRUE,

WHY DO GOOD PEOPLE SUFFER WHILE THE WICKED SEEM TO HAVE AN EASY LIFE?

YEAH! THAT DOESN'T SEEM FAIR!

HMM, THAT'S SOMETHING WE ALL WONDER ABOUT!

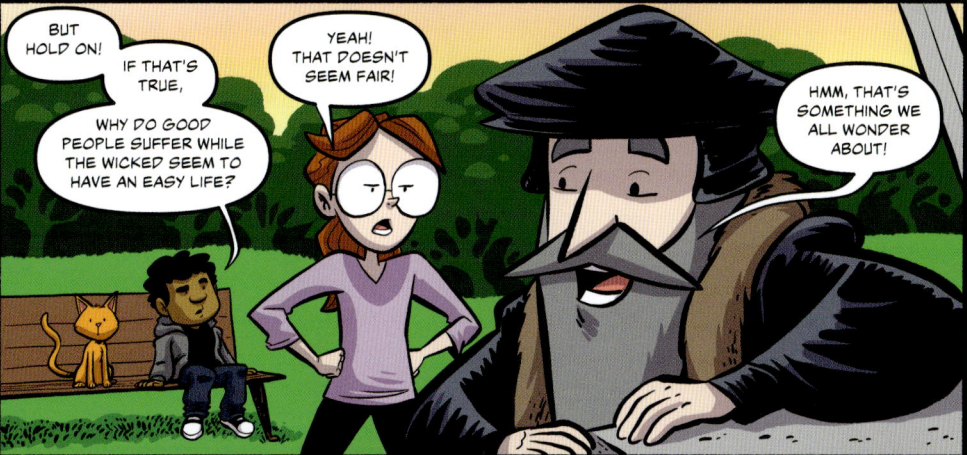

WHY DOESN'T GOD JUST PUNISH THE WICKED RIGHT AWAY?

BECAUSE GOD IS PERFECTLY JUST,

WE CAN TRUST THAT A FINAL JUDGMENT IS COMING.

ON THAT DAY, THE WICKED WILL BE PUNISHED, AND THE RIGHTEOUS WILL BE REWARDED.

SO, MR. CALVIN, WHAT'S THE PURPOSE OF GOD'S WORK IN CREATION AND PROVIDENCE?

GOD'S PURPOSE IS THAT WE MIGHT COME TO KNOW HIM, LOVE HIM, AND WORSHIP HIM.

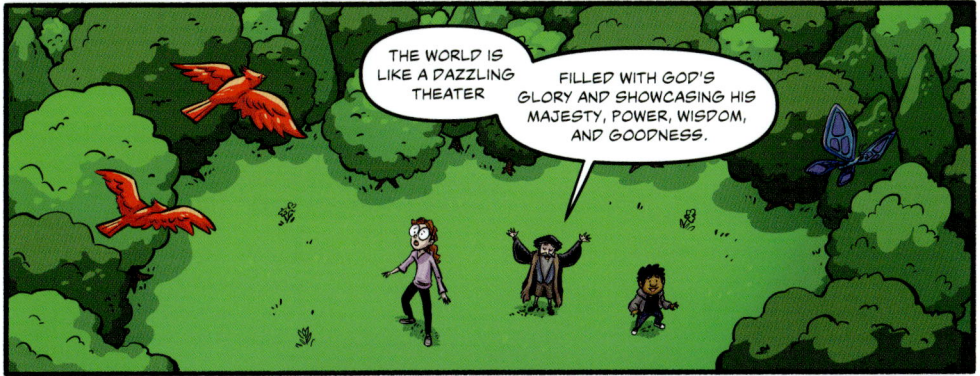

THE WORLD IS LIKE A DAZZLING THEATER

FILLED WITH GOD'S GLORY AND SHOWCASING HIS MAJESTY, POWER, WISDOM, AND GOODNESS.

BUT EVEN THOUGH GOD'S GLORY SHINES ALL AROUND US,

PEOPLE CAN'T SEE IT BECAUSE SIN HAS BLINDED THEIR HEARTS.

THE PROBLEM ISN'T A LACK OF LIGHT BUT THE DARKNESS AND CORRUPTION **WITHIN** THE HUMAN HEART.

PEOPLE ARE FULLY RESPONSIBLE FOR THEIR SIN. IT'S THEIR FAULT ALONE THAT THEY DON'T KNOW, LOVE, AND WORSHIP GOD AS THEY SHOULD.
THAT'S WHY THE APOSTLE PAUL SAYS IN ROMANS 1:20:
"THEY ARE WITHOUT EXCUSE!"
BUT DON'T DESPAIR.
HOPE IS ON THE HORIZON.

God has planted a "seed of religion" in every human heart so that we might know him, love him, and find true happiness in him. God has also revealed himself to us through creation, which serves as a dazzling theater that displays his majesty, power, wisdom, and goodness. From the vast heavens to the intricate human body, every part of creation reflects his glory. Yet out of all creation, humanity is God's masterpiece—we are fearfully and wonderfully made and offer living proof of the wisdom and power of our Creator.

God additionally reveals himself through his providence—his rule over all creation and human history. He not only created the world but actively upholds and rules it with perfect wisdom, justice, and mercy. Nothing happens by chance; God commands the seas, orders the planets, changes the seasons, and provides for all creatures. Every event unfolds according to his holy, loving, and just will.

Though the wicked may prosper and the righteous suffer in this life, God's justice will ultimately triumph. In his mercy, God delays judgment in order to give sinners the opportunity to repent. Thus, by governing all things with perfect wisdom and purpose, God reveals himself not only as a just Judge but also as a merciful Father.

The purpose of God's creation and providence is to lead humanity to know, love, and glorify him. But although God clearly reveals himself through his creation and his providence, sin blinds humanity to his glory. The problem is not a lack of evidence; it is the darkness and corruption within the human heart. His majesty, justice, and mercy are evident in all he has made, yet people refuse to honor or worship him as they should. Thus, as Paul writes in Romans 1:20, "They are without excuse."

READ CALVIN FOR YOURSELF!
BOOK 1, CHAPTER 5, SECTIONS 1-15

1. What does Calvin mean when he says that we find true happiness in knowing and enjoying God? How does this challenge the way people often seek happiness?

2. How do the universe, the natural world, and the human body reflect God's majesty, power, and wisdom? How can thinking about the beauty and complexity of creation help you worship him more deeply?

3. What does Calvin say God's providence is? How does recognizing the wisdom and justice with which he governs the world comfort us amid life's chaos? Can you think of a specific moment when you saw God's hand in your life?

4. How does the story of Joseph, found in Genesis 37; 39–50, display God's providence? What does Joseph mean when he says, "You meant evil against me, but God meant it for good" (Genesis 50:20)? How does his conclusion shape our understanding of God's control over human actions?

5. We most clearly see the providence of God in Christ's death and resurrection, as Peter points out in Acts 4:23–28. What does this teach us about God's purpose for history?

6. How can God's promise of final judgment help us cope with injustice in the present, and what can help believers trust in God's justice during times of suffering?

7. Calvin says that sin blinds us to the glory of God revealed in creation and providence. What are some specific ways that sin hinders your ability to see God's glory in the world or in your life? What can you do to overcome this blindness?

8. How does God's revelation support the apostle Paul's teaching that all are "without excuse" (Romans 1:20)? What do both creation and providence indicate about our responsibility for our actions and sins?

9. Think of a scientific or medical discovery that you've heard about recently. What does it tell you about God that might deepen your worship of him? What are the dangers of neglecting to honor God while we study his creation?

10. God's purpose in creation and providence is to lead us to know, love, and worship him. What practical steps can you take this week to do so?